WITHDRAWN

CELL SYSTEMS

Lori McManus

Heinemann
LIBRARY

Chicago, Illinois

www.heinemannraintree.com
Visit our website to find out more information about Heinemann-Raintree books.

To order:
☎ Phone 888-454-2279
⌨ Visit www.heinemannraintree.com to browse our catalog and order online.

© 2011 Heinemann Library
an imprint of Capstone Global Library, LLC
Chicago, Illinois

Visit our website at www.heinemannraintree.com

Edited by Megan Cotugno and Andrew Farrow
Designed by Philippa Jenkins
Original illustrations © Capstone Global Library, Ltd.
Illustrated by KJA-artists.com
Picture research by Hannah Taylor
Production by Alison Parsons
Originated by Capstone Global Library, Ltd.
Printed by Leo Paper Products, Ltd.

14 13 12 11 10
10 9 8 7 6 5 4 3 2 1

Library of Congress Cataloging-in-Publication Data
McManus, Lori.
  Cell systems / Lori McManus.
    p. cm. -- (Investigating cells)
  Includes bibliographical references and index.
  ISBN 978-1-4329-3879-6 (hc)
 1. Life (Biology)--Juvenile literature. 2. Organisms--Juvenile literature. 3. Organs (Anatomy)--Juvenile literature. 4. Cells--Juvenile literature. I. Title.
  QH501.M38 2011
  570--dc22
                          2009049974

Acknowledgments
The author and publishers are grateful to the following for permission to reproduce copyright material: ©Alamy Images pp. 19 (©The Art Gallery Collection), 23 (©UpperCut Images), 39 (©Kevin Schafer), 40 (©Grant Heilman Photography); ©Corbis p. 8 (Nick Turchiaro); ©Photolibrary pp. 4 (Doc White), 21 (Medicimage), 28 (Scott Camazine), 41 (George Ostertag), 42 (Garry Delong), 43 (Dennis Kunkel); ©Science Photo Library pp. 6, 12 (Eye of Science), 13 (Southern Illinois University), 14 (Morris Huberland), 17 (Medi-mation), 18 (Eye of Science), 24 (Gary Carlson), 25 (Arthur Glauberman), 27 (Steve Gschmessiener), 29 (Simon Fraser), 30 (Medical RF.com), 33 (Joti), 34 (Steve Gschmessiener), 35 (Steve Gschmessiener), 36 (Dr Gopal Murti), 37; ©shutterstock p. 7 (©Christopher Dodge).

Cover photograph of human lungs reproduced with the permission of Science Photo Library (Pasieka).

We would like to thank Michelle Raabe, Ph.D., for her invaluable help in the preparation of this book.

Contents

Some words are printed in bold, **like this**. You can find out what they mean by looking in the glossary.

What Is an Organism?

An **organism** is any living thing. The largest animal in the world, the blue whale, is an organism. Smaller animals like dogs, birds, and bees are also organisms. Rose bushes, apple trees, and humans fit into this category, too. Anything on Earth that is alive is an organism.

All animals are organisms, from the largest whale, to the smallest flea.

How can we tell if something is living?

All organisms have seven characteristics in common. These characteristics are called **life processes**. Only something that does all seven life processes is considered a living thing.

SEVEN LIFE PROCESSES		
1	Movement	All living things move parts of their bodies, or they move their bodies as a whole.
2	Reproduction	All living things produce more of their kind.
3	Sensitivity	All living things react to change in their surroundings.
4	Nutrition	All living things need food to stay alive.
5	Excretion	All living things get rid of **waste** (leftover) materials.
6	Respiration	All living things turn food into energy.
7	Growth	All living things grow larger and more complex over time.

An easy way to remember these seven life processes is by using the first letter of each process. Together, the letters spell "**MRS NERG.**"

Plants and animals

Plants and animals do all seven life processes. For example, a cat races across the street (movement) to avoid being hit by a car (sensitivity) on its way to eat a meal (nutrition). The cat gains energy from the food (**respiration**) so that it can play with its kittens, which were born six weeks before (**reproduction**). The kittens have grown rapidly since birth (growth) and have already learned to use the litter box as a toilet (excretion). Although other plants and animals may not be as obvious as the cat, each one is an organism because it does all seven life processes.

Do other organisms exist?

Plants and animals are not the only organisms on Earth. Fungi and **bacteria** are also living things. Organisms like mold, mildew, and mushrooms are examples of fungi. Bacteria are extremely small organisms that can cause sickness. But bacteria can also be useful for **digestion**, the process by which food is broken down into materials the body can use. Fungi and bacteria qualify as organisms because they do all of the seven life processes.

What are organisms made of?

All organisms are made of tiny units called **cells**. Most cells are too small to see without a microscope. Some organisms, like bacteria, are made up of just one cell. Other organisms are made of many cells. A human body has between 50 and 100 trillion cells. A trillion is a million million! Living things made of two or more cells are called multicellular organisms.

Viewed with an electron microscope, these flat cells make up the outer layer of human skin.

How Does an Organism Work?

An **organism** works because of the systems inside it. A system is a set of parts that interact with one another in an orderly way, so that the entire machine runs well. For example, a car's engine works together with the steering system to move the vehicle forward. In order to stop, the car also has a brake system. Each of these systems is made of smaller parts, like the steering wheel, tires, and brake pedal. The systems interact with each other to make it possible to drive a car.

Organ systems and organs

Animals are also made of systems. These **organ systems** cooperate to make the seven **life processes** possible. Each organ system has two or more different parts, called organs, that work together to complete a specific job. For instance, the heart works together with the blood and the **blood vessels** to carry oxygen around the body.

A sports car runs smoothly when all of its parts and systems interact with each other in an organized way. This is also true of the human body.

Tissues

An animal's organs are made up of even smaller parts, called **tissues**. Tissues are sheets of **cells** joined together. An organ is made up of two or more tissues that work together to perform a particular job. For example, the heart has **muscle tissue** so that it can pump blood and **epithelial tissue** for protection. These tissues cooperate so that the heart can do its job of moving oxygen around the body. (See pages 34–35 for more about these tissues.)

Cells that make up tissues

Tissues are made up of two or more different kinds of cells. Each type of cell in your body performs a special job so that the entire tissue works correctly. The muscle tissue of the heart is made of both cardiac muscle cells and other cells. These different cells cooperate so that the muscle tissue can pump hard, but also remain stable.

Teamwork

Each organ system is absolutely necessary for all seven life processes to work. The different systems must also communicate and cooperate with each other. Your body needs its system for breathing to interact with the system that carries gases around the body. Communication among organ systems allows your body to work better than it would if each system did its own job separately.

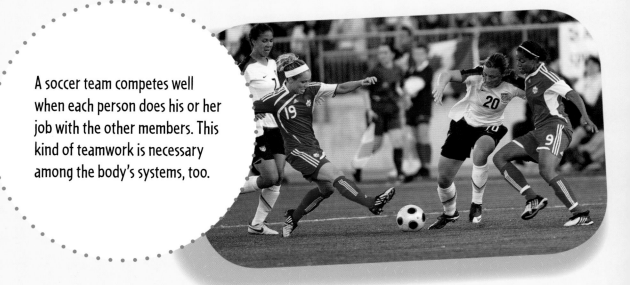

A soccer team competes well when each person does his or her job with the other members. This kind of teamwork is necessary among the body's systems, too.

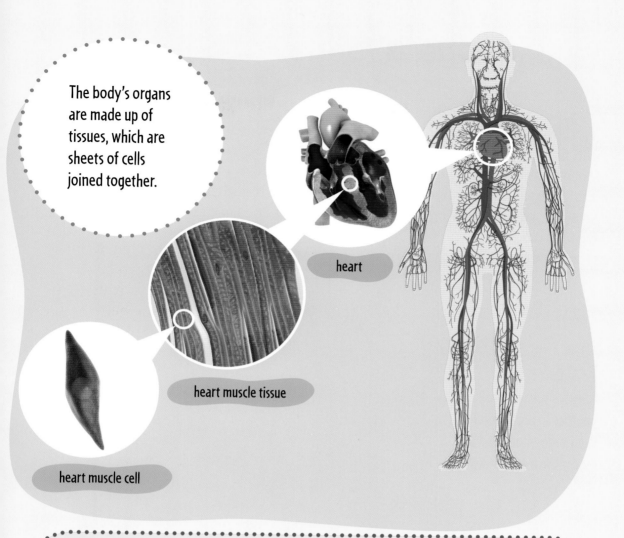

The body's organs are made up of tissues, which are sheets of cells joined together.

heart

heart muscle tissue

heart muscle cell

What Happens to the Food We Eat?

The human body has an **organ system** specifically designed to break down the food we eat. The **digestive system** is made up of **organs** that help turn food into very small, usable **nutrients**. Nutrients are chemicals needed for growth and energy. The digestive system starts with the mouth, where the biting, chewing, and swallowing of food takes place. It ends with an organ called the large intestine. Each organ along the way is made of **tissues** and **cells** that do important jobs so the body can use food for energy.

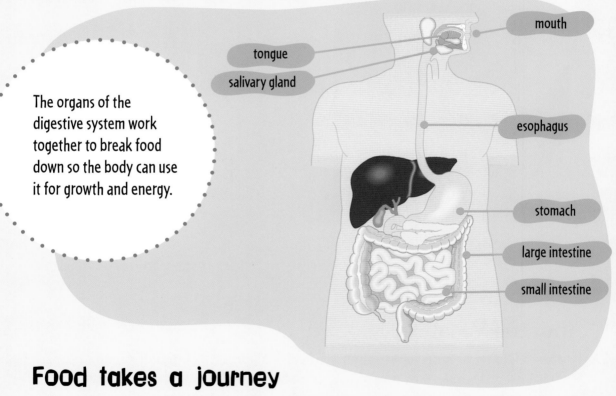

The organs of the digestive system work together to break food down so the body can use it for growth and energy.

mouth

tongue

salivary gland

esophagus

stomach

large intestine

small intestine

Food takes a journey

When you take a bite of an apple, the organs of the digestive system are ready to work. Inside the mouth, the teeth are used to break down the food into smaller pieces. Saliva, or spit, helps make the food mushy and easier to swallow. The tongue has a job, too. It pushes food around so that the teeth can do the work of chewing. The tongue also pushes small amounts of mushy food to the back of the throat so that it can be swallowed.

Where does the food go next?

After it leaves the mouth, food enters the esophagus, a stretchy pipe that connects the mouth to the stomach. The walls of the esophagus contain **muscle tissues** that move in waves. These waves squeeze food through the esophagus into the stomach. Because the esophagus uses muscles, the chewed-up food would still get to the stomach even if you were standing on your head!

What does saliva do?

You produce a lot of saliva each day—about 1 to 2 liters (4 to 8 cups)! Saliva helps break down the chemicals in food. Saliva also breaks down food caught in between teeth, protecting the teeth from decay. It does this with the help of something called **enzymes**. Enzymes are substances that speed up chemical changes in the body.

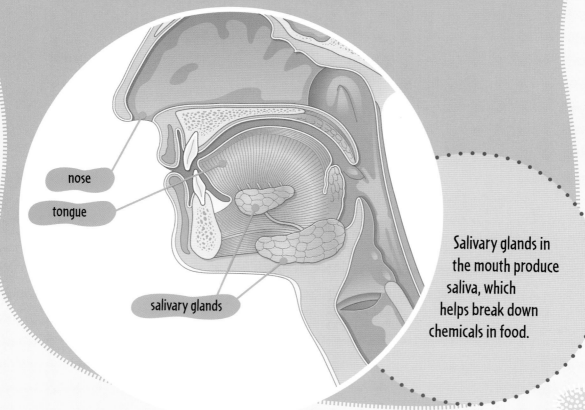

nose

tongue

salivary glands

Salivary glands in the mouth produce saliva, which helps break down chemicals in food.

What happens in the stomach?

The stomach is a stretchy pink organ with three special jobs:

1. To store food that has been eaten
2. To break down food into a liquid mixture
3. To empty this liquid mixture slowly into the small intestine.

The stomach works like an electric mixer, mashing and churning the bits of food into smaller and smaller pieces. The stomach walls produce a **mucus** (slippery, sticky substance) containing acids that help turn the food into liquid. Then, the chemicals in the food can be used by the body.

Mucus cells line the inside of the stomach. These cells produce mucus, or "slime," to help with digestion.

When empty, the sides of the stomach squeeze together to make a wrinkled surface, as seen in this photo. With food inside, the surface of the stomach swells and becomes smooth.

A closer look at the stomach

The stomach is a complex organ, containing four different types of tissues that work together to break down food. The outer lining of the stomach is made of **epithelial tissue** that protects the stomach and keeps its contents inside. Next are three layers of **muscle tissue** that enable the stomach to mix and mash the food. The stomach walls also contain **connective tissue** and **nerve tissue**, so that the stomach maintains its shape and communicates with other organs. The innermost layer of the stomach is covered with a squishy epithelial tissue.

Amazingly, each type of tissue in the stomach is made up of different kinds of cells. These cells work together so the tissue can do its job. For instance, the squishy epithelial tissue that lines the stomach is made of four types of cells. Three of these cells produce the acids and juices that break down food. The fourth kind, the mucous cell, produces the mucus that protects the stomach wall from its own acids and juices. The mucous cells make a new lining every few days to prevent the stomach from digesting itself!

What does the small intestine do?

The liquid food from the stomach empties slowly into the small intestine. The small intestine is a stretchy tube that folds up underneath the stomach. This important organ adds more juices to the liquid food mixture to make it thinner. It also adds enzymes and **hormones**, chemicals that carry messages and help control how tissues and organs do their work. These added ingredients break down the food into extremely small pieces called **molecules**.

The mixture becomes so thin that it can pass from the intestine into the blood. The blood can then use the small particles (bits) of vitamins, **minerals**, **proteins** (molecules that build tissues), **fats** (molecules that store energy), and sugars from the food to give the body energy for all seven **life processes**. Water is also absorbed into the blood from the small intestine.

A few other organs

The pancreas, liver, and gallbladder have jobs in the digestive system, too. These organs send different juices to the upper part of the small intestine. These juices help the process of **digestion**. They also allow the body to absorb nutrients from the food.

The liver is a very important organ. In addition to helping with digestion, it performs other jobs, including breaking down harmful substances and storing vitamins.

Last stop

Eventually, the remaining food passes into the large intestine. This stretchy tube is larger, but also shorter, than the small intestine. Any remaining water in the food passes from the large intestine into the blood. The parts of the food that cannot be used, called **waste**, get harder and drier. The waste passes out of the body as feces, or solid waste.

Sizing up the intestines

If an adult's small intestine were stretched out, it would measure about 7 meters (22 feet) from end to end! Although it is long, the small intestine gets its name from its small diameter (measurement across) when compared to the large intestine. The small intestine is about 3 centimeters (1.2 inches) wide, while the large intestine measures about 7 to 10 centimeters (3 to 4 inches) across. The average length of an adult's large intestine is 1.5 meters (5 feet).

Food takes between three and six hours to pass from one end of the small intestine to the other.

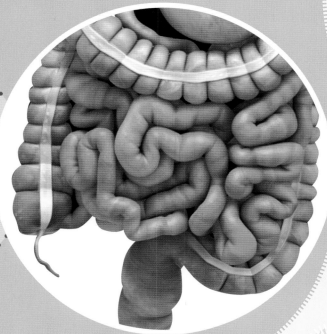

How Do Things Get Around Inside an Organism?

Once the **digestive system** has broken down food into liquid **nutrients**, those nutrients pass into another **organ system**. The **circulatory system** transports these nutrients around the body. Gases, water, and chemicals also move around the body through this system. The primary job of the circulatory system is to deliver materials to the places they need to go.

The circulatory system contains three main parts: the heart, **blood vessels**, and blood. The heart pumps blood to every part of the body through organized rubbery tubes called blood vessels. The blood delivers oxygen and nutrients to **organs**, **tissues**, and **cells**. As the blood returns to the heart, it picks up **waste** materials like carbon dioxide so the body can get rid of them.

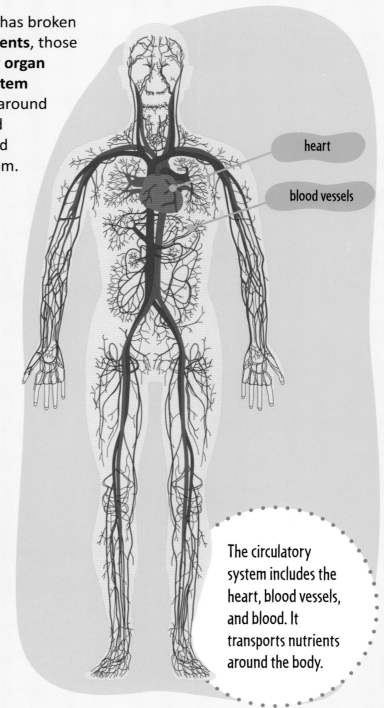

heart

blood vessels

The circulatory system includes the heart, blood vessels, and blood. It transports nutrients around the body.

The work of the heart

The heart is an amazing organ about the size of your fist. It is a muscle that works like a pump. The left side of the heart pushes blood full of nutrients and oxygen out to all parts of the body. The right side of the heart receives blood back from the body. The right side then pumps the blood into the lungs to remove carbon dioxide it has picked up during its journey.

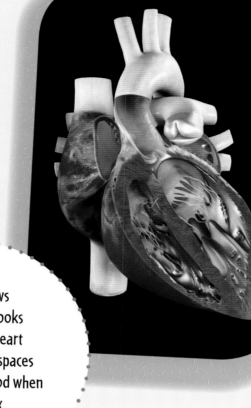

This picture shows what the heart looks like inside. The heart contains hollow spaces that fill with blood when the muscles relax.

What is the beat?

The heart "beats" every time the muscle **contracts**, or squeezes together, to push the blood out and around the body. When you are resting, your heart beats around 70 times per minute. The number of beats increases when you exercise. Your heart will beat approximately 2.5 billion times during your life!

Blood vessels

Blood does not just slosh around in the body. Once blood leaves the heart, it travels through the blood vessels. Blood vessels have many small branches to make sure all the cells in the body get the materials they need from the blood. The blood vessels that carry blood away from the heart are called arteries. Blood vessels that return blood to the heart are called veins.

What is blood, anyway?

Blood carries and delivers materials the body needs to survive. Blood is made up of three parts—plasma, cells, and **proteins**. Plasma is the liquid part of the blood. The rest of the blood is made up of three types of cells:

1. Red blood cells are shaped like flattened doughnuts. These cells deliver oxygen to all parts of the body and then take away carbon dioxide.

2. White blood cells look like round, bumpy balls. They fight disease by killing germs.

3. Platelets are cell fragments, or tiny cells. They help form blood clots when the body gets cut, so that the bleeding stops quickly.

An average person has a little less than 5 liters (about 5 quarts) of blood inside his or her body. A drop of blood moves through the entire circulatory system in just one minute!

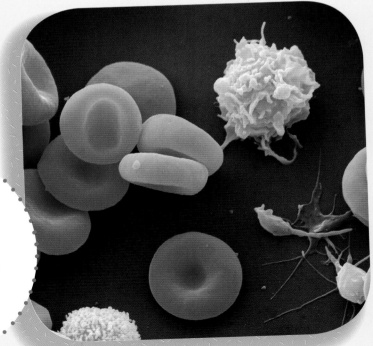

These blood cells are shown 5,600 times larger than their actual size. The green cells are platelets.

Scientist Spotlight

William Harvey

In 1628 English doctor William Harvey (1578–1657) published a book that accurately showed how the circulatory system works. Before Harvey's book, doctors believed that the liver made new blood from the food we eat. By conducting experiments with animals and humans, Harvey discovered the role of the heart, arteries, and veins in moving blood around the body. Harvey gave other doctors and scientists an example of how to learn about the body by performing careful experiments.

William Harvey discovered how the circulatory system works by performing careful experiments.

Does Blood Get Dirty?

As blood travels around the body, it picks up **waste** from **cells**. The body must have a way to remove these chemicals and extra fluids from the blood. The **urinary system**, also called the excretory system, **filters** (separates) and gets rid of waste.

The kidneys

During its journey around the body, blood passes through the two kidneys. The kidneys filter the blood so that it contains just the right amount of chemicals and liquids. The kidneys remove waste from cells as well as extra amounts of water, salt, vitamins, and **minerals**. In the process of filtering the blood, the kidneys produce a liquid called urine.

Ureters, bladder, and urethra

Once urine is made in the kidneys, it drips down two tubes called ureters into a stretchy **organ** known as the bladder. The bladder expands as it stores urine. When the bladder is full, it sends a message to your brain. That is when you need to use a toilet. The muscles around the bladder start squeezing. The circle of muscles at the bottom of the bladder open, and the urine exits your body through an opening called the urethra. All the waste and extra materials filtered from your blood leave with the urine.

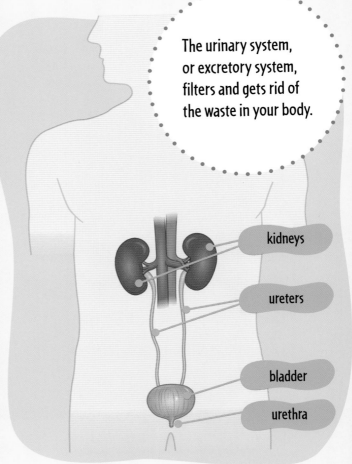

The urinary system, or excretory system, filters and gets rid of the waste in your body.

kidneys

ureters

bladder

urethra

Kidney problems

If the kidneys have a disease, they will not work properly. Waste materials build up in the blood and make the person sick. Kidney disease can be caused by other illnesses, such as diabetes, or by long-term use of certain medicines or illegal drugs.

Constant cleaning

Because the **circulatory system** is constantly moving blood around the body, the kidneys filter your blood hundreds of times each day. Approximately 180 liters (48 gallons) of blood flow through the kidneys every 24 hours!

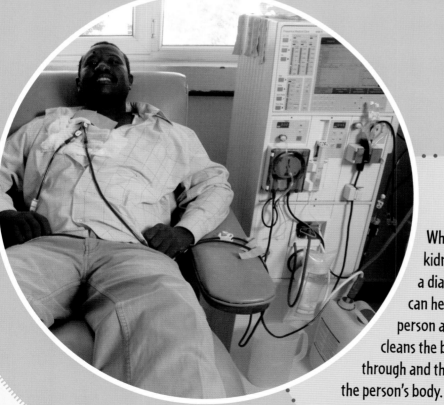

When a person's kidneys stop working, a dialysis machine can help keep the person alive. This machine cleans the blood as it passes through and then returns it to the person's body.

How Does Breathing Work?

Breathing air is possible because of the **respiratory system**. This **organ system** involves the nose, mouth, and lungs, along with a few other **organs**. The job of the respiratory system is to provide blood with oxygen to keep the body's **cells** alive. The respiratory system also gets rid of a dangerous gas called carbon dioxide.

The nose, mouth, and trachea

The respiratory system starts with the nose and mouth. A person takes in air from the environment through these two organs. The air then moves down the trachea, or windpipe. This tube connects the nose and mouth to the lungs. The trachea actually splits into two tubes at the lower end. The air leaves these tubes and travels through smaller tubes into the lungs.

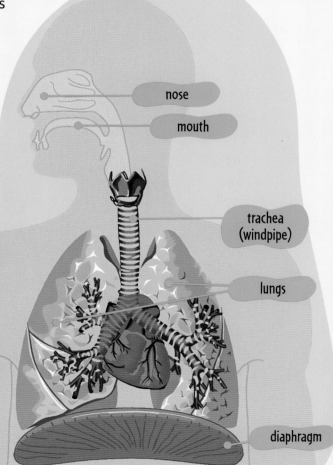

nose

mouth

trachea (windpipe)

lungs

diaphragm

Air enters the respiratory system through the nose and mouth, then travels down the trachea and into the lungs.

The lungs

The biggest organ in the respiratory system is the lungs. Humans have two lungs, located inside the chest. You can feel the lungs in action when you take in a deep breath. Your chest will get slightly bigger. When you release the air, or exhale, your chest returns to a normal size. The important job of the lungs is to transfer oxygen from the air to the blood, and then to take carbon dioxide out of the blood so that it can be exhaled into the environment.

The diaphragm

The body needs muscles to make breathing work. The diaphragm is a large, flat muscle underneath the lungs. The diaphragm and other muscles help push air in and out of the lungs. These muscles make breathing happen without you even thinking about it. In fact, adults take about 12 to 20 breaths a minute—even when they are sleeping!

With a deep breath, the diaphragm tightens and moves downward. This makes room for the lungs to expand as they fill with air.

A closer look at the lungs

Air that enters the lungs from the trachea does not just ooze oxygen into the bloodstream. Instead, it travels into the lungs through smaller tubes attached to the trachea. Once inside the lungs, the oxygen moves along an organized network of even smaller tubes called bronchi and bronchioles. Small air sacs called alveoli are located at the end of the tubes. Oxygen **molecules** pass through the thin walls of the alveoli into the blood. Carbon dioxide passes from the blood into the alveoli.

The lungs are a spongelike organ made of several types of **tissues** that work together. The bronchioles are lined with smooth **muscle tissue** that helps move air through the passageway. **Connective tissue** helps the bronchioles maintain their tubelike shape. Additionally, bronchioles are lined with an **epithelial tissue** that traps and gets rid of pollutants like dust, which can cause harm to the body.

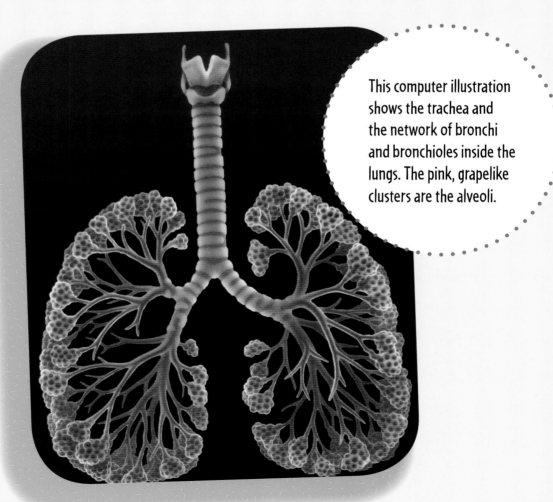

This computer illustration shows the trachea and the network of bronchi and bronchioles inside the lungs. The pink, grapelike clusters are the alveoli.

Living with asthma

Asthma is a disease of the respiratory system that does not go away like a cold or flu. Asthma causes the bronchial tubes to become narrow and sore. Since these tubes carry air to the lungs, asthma makes breathing difficult. Asthma cannot be cured, but it can be helped with medicines.

Problems in the respiratory system

Have you experienced a stuffy nose and sore throat this year? These signs indicate an **infection** in the respiratory system. Common respiratory infections include colds and influenza (flu). Colds and flu have signs and symptoms affecting the mouth, nose, and throat. These are caused by viruses, which are small germs that invade the body's cells.

Infections caused by **bacteria** tend to concentrate in just one area of the respiratory system. For example, a bacterial infection in the bronchial tubes is called bronchitis. When the infection is in the lungs, it is called pneumonia. Bacterial infections are more common in smokers, people who breathe secondhand smoke, and people with previous lung problems.

The lung on the left is healthy, while the lung on the right shows the damage caused by smoking.

How Do Bodies Keep a Regular Shape?

If you did not have bones, you would be floppy like a beanbag. Bones, ligaments, and cartilage make up the **organ system** that gives your body a regular shape. This system, called the **skeletal system**, has five main jobs:

1. *To provide structure so the body maintains its shape.* The solid framework of the bones provides places for the softer **organs** and **tissues** of the body to attach.

2. *To protect the important organs inside the body.* For example, your rib cage protects the heart, lungs, liver, and stomach. Your skull acts like a helmet around the brain.

3. *To help with movement.* Muscles attach to bones and make the body move.

4. *To help with storage.* The skeletal system stores important **minerals** as well as **fats**.

5. *To help with blood cell formation.*

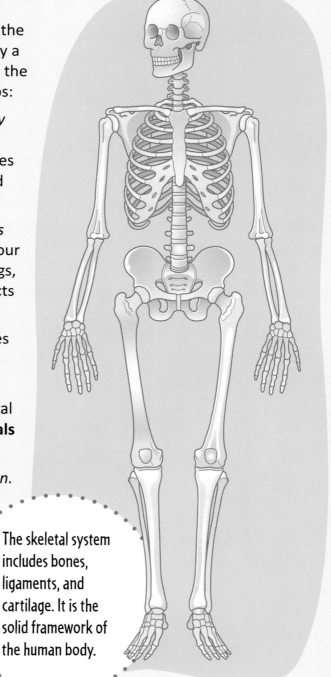

The skeletal system includes bones, ligaments, and cartilage. It is the solid framework of the human body.

Bones

Bones are organs that contain living cells. Almost all bones in the body are made of the same set of tissues. The outer layer of the bone is a thin **membrane** (layer of tissue) that contains **blood vessels** and **nerves**, which are cords that carry messages to and from the brain. The blood vessels carry **nutrients** from the blood to the bone.

The next layer, called compact bone tissue, is smooth, hard, and very strong. A layer in the middle of the bone, called spongy bone, contains bone marrow. Bone marrow looks like thick jelly and has the important job of making new blood cells.

A bone's hard outer layer surrounds the spongy red bone marrow inside.

What is cartilage?

Cartilage is a **connective tissue** that provides structure and support in the skeletal system. Cartilage is not as hard as bone, but it is stiffer than muscle. Cartilage can be found in many areas of the skeleton, including the nose, the ear, and the knee. Wiggle your nose with your hand to feel the hardness and flexibility of cartilage.

What are joints?

Joints are the places where two bones meet. Some joints in the body move, while others do not. The skull is made of different bones that meet together so that they are fixed permanently in certain positions.

Joints that move allow your body to jump, twist, or throw a baseball. For example, the joint at your elbow allows you to bend and straighten your arm. Bones are held together at moving joints by ligaments, which are like strong rubber bands.

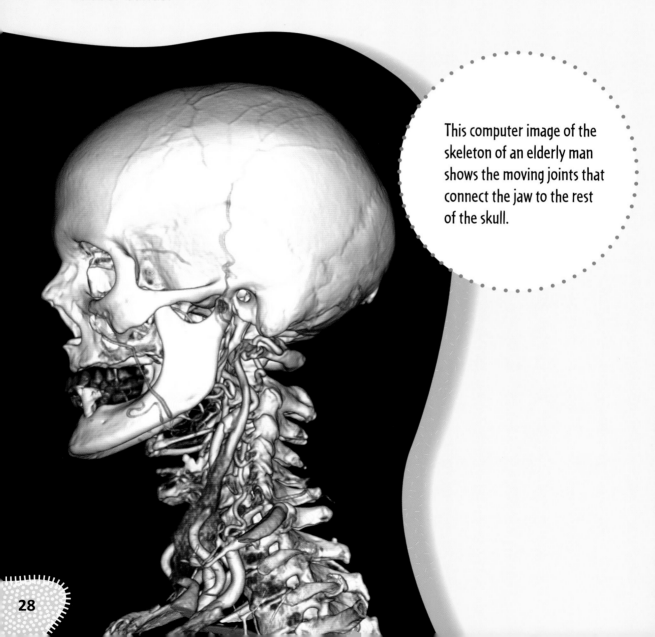

This computer image of the skeleton of an elderly man shows the moving joints that connect the jaw to the rest of the skull.

Scientist Spotlight

Raymond Damadian

Armenian-American medical doctor and research scientist Raymond Damadian (born 1936) built the world's first whole-body MRI scanner. MRI (short for "magnetic resonance imaging") uses the force of magnets and radio waves to take clear pictures of the body's internal organs. In 1970 Damadian figured out that MRI could be used to find cancer in animals, including humans. His next step was to build a machine that used this technology to look inside the entire body at once. This kind of scanner would help doctors see problems without having to use surgery or X-rays.

For seven years, Damadian and two other doctors, Dr. Larry Minkoff and Dr. Michael Goldsmith, worked diligently on this machine. In 1977 the whole-body MRI scanner was used for the first time. It took five hours to produce just one picture, but it worked successfully! For his invention, Damadian received a National Medal of Technology. Damadian's original MRI machine is now in the Smithsonian Institution in Washington, DC. MRI scans continue to be used by doctors as a reliable and safe way to take pictures of internal organs.

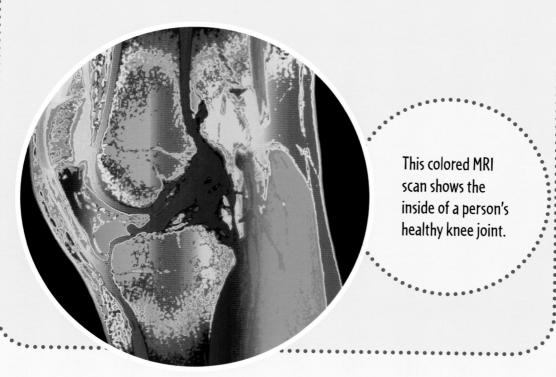

This colored MRI scan shows the inside of a person's healthy knee joint.

How Do We Bend and Move?

Muscles help humans to move in all kinds of ways, including skipping, hopping, kicking, twirling, and dancing. The human body contains more than 600 muscles. Different types of muscles work together to form the **muscular system**.

Skeletal muscles look striated (striped) because they are made of fibers, or strong threads, that have light and dark parts.

How do muscles work?

Muscles only pull in one direction. They cannot push. Often muscles work together in pairs so that they can pull in opposite directions. This is how you are able to wiggle your fingers and toes back and forth. In order to make the pulling movement, the **cells** inside a muscle tighten up, or **contract**. Then the cells relax back to their regular size.

Are all muscles the same?

The human body has three different types of muscles:

1. skeletal muscle
2. smooth muscle
3. cardiac muscle.

The muscles that you control are called skeletal muscles. You use skeletal muscles to talk, run, raise an eyebrow, and write your name. Skeletal muscles are connected to the bones in your body with tendons. Tendons are cords made of tough **tissue**. When the muscle moves, the tendon and the attached bone move with it.

Automatic movement

Smooth muscle is the kind of muscle that moves automatically. Your brain tells these muscles to move without you having to think about it. Smooth muscles cause your eyes to blink. The diaphragm is made of skeletal muscle that acts like smooth muscle, which allows you to continue breathing even while you sleep. Smooth muscles also help the intestines move your food along.

What about muscle in the heart?

Cardiac muscle is a special kind of muscle found only in the heart. Cardiac muscle moves by itself without any help from you. When the muscles of the heart contract, blood is pumped out and around the body. Blood flows back into the heart when the muscles relax.

Are There More Organ Systems?

Humans have 11 **organ systems** in all. Just like the systems already mentioned, the 5 remaining organ systems do specific work in the body. The following chart shows the name of each system, the important job of that system, and the specific **organs** that are involved in performing that job.

SYSTEM	MAIN JOB	ORGANS
digestive	To break down food and absorb **nutrients**	mouth, esophagus, stomach, small intestine, large intestine, liver, pancreas, gallbladder
circulatory	To transport materials around the body through the blood and defend against disease	heart, **blood vessels**, blood
urinary	To get rid of **waste** materials, including salt	kidneys, ureters, bladder, urethra
respiratory	To provide the body with oxygen and get rid of carbon dioxide	nose, mouth, trachea, lungs, bronchi, bronchioles
skeletal	To provide support, shape, and protection for the body; also to help with movement, storage, and blood-**cell** formation	bones, cartilage, ligaments
muscular	To provide movement and keep the body steady; also to provide body heat	muscles, tendons
nervous	To send, receive, and respond to messages from the body's external and internal environment	brain, spinal cord, **nerves**; sense organs such as eyes and ears
endocrine	To control growth, development, metabolism (the chemical actions that keep cells alive), and **reproduction** by releasing **hormones**	**glands** (groups of cells that make a product) that produce hormones, including pituitary, thyroid, and adrenal
reproductive	To provide the cells, hormones, and body parts necessary to create babies	In females: ovaries, uterus, vagina; in males: testes, prostate gland, penis
immune/ lymphatic	To protect the body from diseases; also to return **tissue** fluid to the body	lymph nodes, lymphatic fluid and vessels, spleen, tonsils
integumentary	To protect the body from the environment; also to control body temperature	skin, hair, nails, sweat glands, oil glands

What is the body's largest organ?

Surprisingly, skin is the body's largest organ! Skin is made of three layers that work together to protect your internal organs and keep **infection** out. The skin also helps keep the body at just the right temperature.

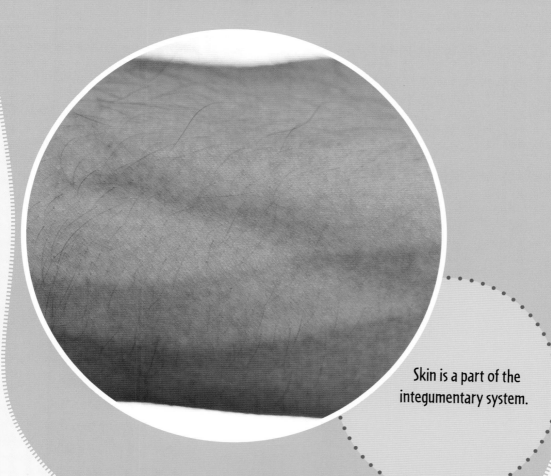

Skin is a part of the integumentary system.

What Kinds of Tissues and Cells Exist?

All **organs** are made of two to four different types of **tissues** working together to perform a special job. The list below shows the names and jobs of the four kinds of tissues within the organs of the human body.

Tissue types:

1. **Connective tissue**: Adds structure and support to organs.

2. **Muscle tissue**: Produces movement.

3. **Epithelial tissue**: Serves as a protective lining.

4. **Nerve tissue**: Sends and receives messages from the brain and environment.

An easy way to remember the four kinds of tissues is by using the first letter of each type to say "**C**lothed **MEN**."

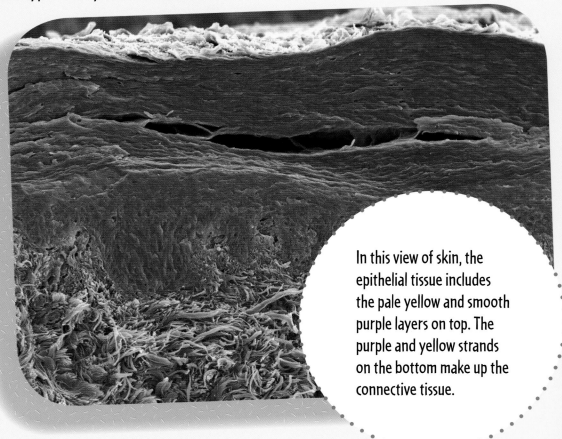

In this view of skin, the epithelial tissue includes the pale yellow and smooth purple layers on top. The purple and yellow strands on the bottom make up the connective tissue.

Cell types

Each body tissue is made of two or more different kinds of **cells**. For example, the connective tissue in bone is made of three special types of cells: osteoblasts, osteocytes, and osteoclasts. The human body contains about 210 different cell types! Each type of cell has a specialized job within a tissue, organ, and **organ system**.

Do all cells look alike?

Cells that perform different jobs have different shapes. For example, neurons (**nerve** cells) have long branches that can send and receive messages. Red blood cells look like flattened doughnuts. The flat area helps these cells pick up and carry oxygen around the body. Each cell's shape matches the job it performs.

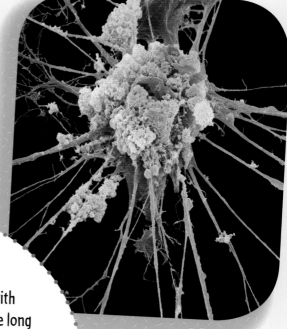

Each neuron has a central core with several treelike branches and one long branch that looks like a cable. The long cable sends messages that are received by the shorter branches of the next cell.

Do all cells have the same parts?

All animal cells, including cells in humans, have four main parts: the nucleus, cytoplasm, **organelles**, and cell **membrane**. The nucleus controls the cell's activities. Cytoplasm contains a gel-like fluid that fills the cell. Organelles are structures that float in the cytoplasm and perform important jobs. The cell membrane controls what materials can get into and out of the cell. Each cell's parts are carefully organized to do work for the body.

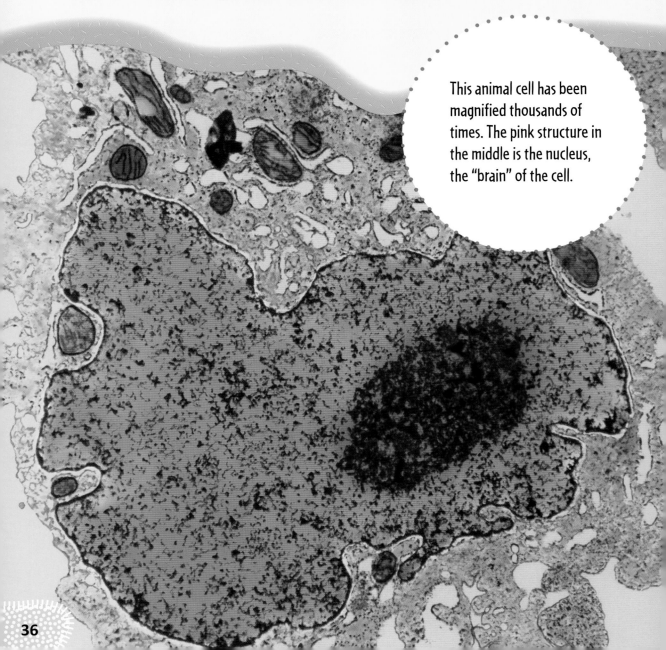

This animal cell has been magnified thousands of times. The pink structure in the middle is the nucleus, the "brain" of the cell.

How are cells made?

Cells can get worn out or damaged by scrapes, cuts, and other injuries. New cells are constantly being made inside the body to replace the old ones. At a certain point in a cell's growth, it divides to make two new cells that are identical to the original. The new cells grow and then divide again. This process of **cell division** is how the body heals itself and keeps tissues working.

Babies and cell division

Cell division also explains how babies are made and how they grow into adults. When a male sperm cell combines with a female egg cell, a single cell called a zygote is formed. Hours after fertilization, the zygote grows and then divides, creating two identical cells. These cells then grow and divide until an entire baby is formed. Along the way, instructions inside the cells make some of them become blood cells, muscle cells, and all the other 210 cell types.

Losing a lot of cells

You lose about 35,000 dead skin cells from the surface of your skin every minute! Underneath, skin cells are constantly growing and dividing so that they can replace the ones that wear out on top.

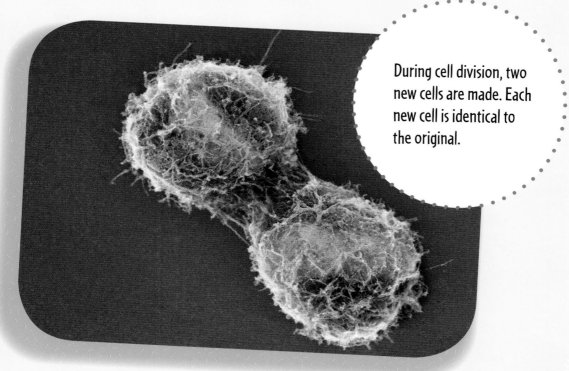

During cell division, two new cells are made. Each new cell is identical to the original.

What Organ Systems Do Other Animals Have?

Most animals on Earth have the same 11 **organ systems** that humans do. This group includes lions, sharks, eagles, lizards, and even insects! However, the size and type of **organs** vary in different animals.

Same organ systems

Vertebrates are animals with backbones. All vertebrates have the same 11 organ systems as humans. Many vertebrates have the same organs, too, although the organs may have different shapes. For example, cows and goats have stomachs with four parts instead of one. And while human hearts have four sections, frog hearts have only three.

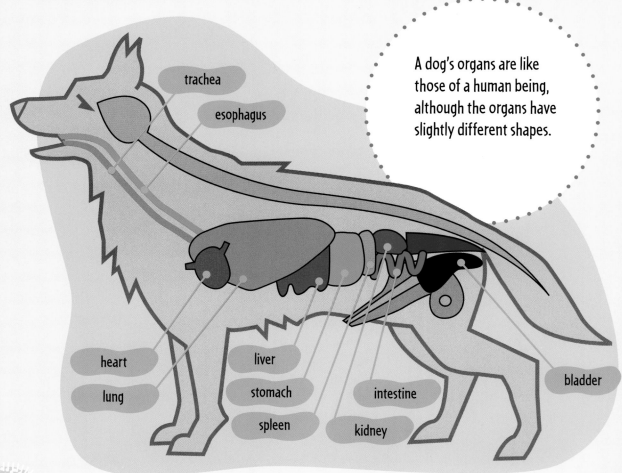

A dog's organs are like those of a human being, although the organs have slightly different shapes.

trachea

esophagus

heart

lung

liver

stomach

spleen

intestine

kidney

bladder

But some vertebrates have different organs entirely, even though they have the same 11 organ systems. For example, fish have gills instead of lungs in their **respiratory system**. A whale breathes air through the blowhole on top of its head rather than through a nose or mouth. Snakes have scales rather than skin for protection from the environment.

What about invertebrates?

Animals without backbones are called invertebrates. Simple invertebrates such as jellyfish have only very primitive (basic) organ systems. Jellyfish do not have a heart, brain, or kidneys. They are organized mostly in **tissues** and **cells**.

But more complex invertebrates, like clams, have the same organ systems as humans. The **digestive system** of a clam includes a mouth, stomach, and intestine. However, some of the clam's organs are very simple. Instead of using **blood vessels**, the blood inside a clam leaves the heart and simply washes over the other organs.

Pacific Sea Nettle Jellyfish are simple invertebrates. They are made of cells and tissues but have very few organs.

How do worms breathe?

Worms breathe through their skin! Worms have **glands** in their skin that produce "slime." The slime keeps the worm's skin moist, so that oxygen can pass in through tiny holes and carbon dioxide can be released. If a worm dries out, it cannot breathe and dies.

Do Plants Have Organ Systems?

Plants have just two **organ systems**. The shoot system includes the parts of the plant that can be seen above ground. The root system extends under the ground.

Shoot system

A plant's shoot system has several important jobs. It makes the plant's food through the process of **photosynthesis**. Photosynthesis is the process of using energy from the Sun to turn carbon dioxide and water into sugars. The shoot system also carries food and water to various **organs**.

The organs of the shoot system are familiar parts of plants: the leaves, stem, flowers, and fruit (if the plant has any). Each organ performs a special job. The stem supports the leaves and flowers. In trees, the stem consists of the trunk and all the branches. The leaves are the main place that photosynthesis takes place. They produce the plant's food, which is carried to other organs by the stem.

The shoot system and the root system interact and communicate to keep the plant healthy.

Root system

A plant's root system has three important jobs:

1. To hold the plant in place.
2. To soak up and transport water and **nutrients**.
3. To store food.

The primary organs of the root system are roots. Roots grow downward toward a source of water. Tiny root hairs cover much of a root's surface. The skin of a root hair allows water and **minerals** to pass in. The plant uses the water and minerals to make food and nourish its **cells**.

Tallest and oldest organisms

The tallest **organism** in the world is a plant! A California redwood can grow to about 111 meters (365 feet) tall and 7 meters (22 feet) across.

A creosote bush, in Lucerne Valley, California, is believed to be the world's oldest plant. Scientists estimate the bush to be 11,700 years old!

A California redwood is the tallest organism on the planet.

Plants have tissues, too

Each plant organ is made of two or three **tissues** working together to get a specific job accomplished. Plants have three types of tissues. The list below gives the name and function of each tissue type:

1. Dermal tissue: Covers the outer surface and prevents water loss.
2. Vascular tissue: Transports materials throughout the plant.
3. Ground tissue: Provides support and storage.

Different types of cells

Each type of plant tissue is made of two or more types of cells. For example, vascular tissue is made of four kinds of cells: xylem, phloem, parenchyma, and cambium. The xylem cells move water and minerals from roots to leaves. Phloem cells transport food from leaves to the rest of the plant. Parenchyma cells provide the bulk of the vascular tissue. In trees, cambium cells make the trunk (stem) thicker by dividing to produce new cells.

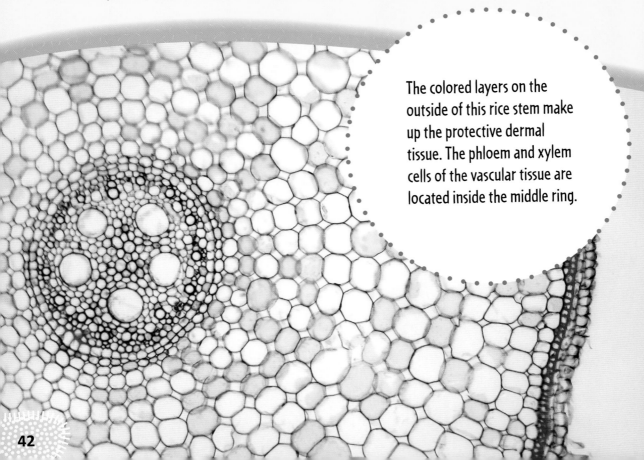

The colored layers on the outside of this rice stem make up the protective dermal tissue. The phloem and xylem cells of the vascular tissue are located inside the middle ring.

Do animal cells and plant cells have the same parts?

Plant cells have the same parts as animal cells, but they also have a few extra structures. The cell wall in a plant cell surrounds the cell **membrane**. The cell wall provides protection and gives the cell a stiff shape. Plant cells also contain chloroplasts. Chloroplasts are special **organelles** that capture light energy to make the plant's food through photosynthesis.

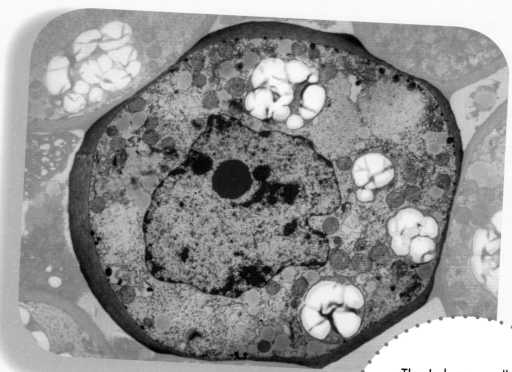

The dark-green cell wall can be seen in this magnified image of a lily plant cell. The cell's nucleus appears light green.

Do all plant cells look alike?

Just like animal cells, plant cells are shaped according to the job they perform. Xylem cells are long and narrow to help them transport water. Guard cells in the dermis tissue are shaped like beans. This shape allows them to control openings in the plant's leaves, stem, and fruit.

Glossary

bacterium (plural: bacteria) extremely small, one-celled organism that can be helpful or harmful

blood vessel rubbery tube that carries blood to and from the heart

cell tiny unit that is the "building block" of all living things

cell division process by which one cell splits to create two identical cells

circulatory system organ system that transports materials around the body through the blood

connective tissue animal tissue that adds structure and support to organs

contract draw or squeeze parts together

digestion process by which food is broken down into materials that can be used by the body

digestive system organ system that breaks down food into small parts that can be used by the body

enzyme substance that increases the rate of chemical reactions in the body

epithelial tissue animal tissue that provides protection

fat soft molecule in food that the body needs for energy storage, digestion of vitamins, and protection against sickness

filter separate and remove parts

gland cell or group of cells that makes a product for use in the body

hormone chemical made in one part of the body and sent to another part of the body to help control how tissues and organs do their work

infection disease resulting from a germ or bacteria

life process task or activity that all living things carry out

membrane thin layer of tissue that serves as a cover or lining

mineral necessary substance like calcium or iron that comes from food, but is made of inorganic material (material that is not from plants or animals)

molecule smallest bit of a substance such as oxygen, calcium, or vitamin C

mucus slippery, sticky substance that moistens and protects

muscle tissue animal tissue that creates movement

muscular system organ system that provides movement and keeps the body steady

nerve bundle of fibers that carries messages to and from the brain

nerve tissue animal tissue that sends and receives messages from the brain and the environment

nutrient chemical that an organism needs to live and grow

organ two or more tissues that carry out a specific job together within the body

organ system two or more organs that work together to perform life processes

organelle structure inside plant and animal cells that performs specific jobs

organism living thing

photosynthesis plant process of using energy from the Sun to change carbon dioxide and water into sugar (plant food) and oxygen

protein molecule from food needed for building and replacing tissues

reproduction process of living things creating more of their kind

respiration process inside cells by which living things get energy from food

respiratory system organ system that provides the body with oxygen and gets rid of carbon dioxide

skeletal system organ system that provides support, shape, and protection for the body

tissue two or more types of cells that work together to perform a specific job

urinary system organ system that gets rid of waste (leftover) materials in the body

waste material that is left over or not needed for use in the body

Find Out More

Books to read

Johnson, Rebecca L. *Mighty Animal Cells*. Minneapolis: Millbrook, 2008.

Johnson, Rebecca L. *Powerful Plant Cells*. Minneapolis: Millbrook, 2008.

Johnson, Rebecca L. *Ultra-Organized Cell Systems*. Minneapolis: Millbrook, 2007.

Petrie, Kristin. *The Digestive System*. Edina, Minn.: Abdo, 2007.

Simon, Seymour. *Guts: Our Digestive System*. New York: Harper Collins, 2005.

Stephens, Nicholas. *Plant Cells and Tissues*. New York: Chelsea House, 2006.

Websites

"Biology 4 Kids!"
http://biology4kids.com
Biology is the study of the ways living things work. This website includes fascinating information on animal systems, cells, plants, and even bacteria.

"How the Body Works"
http://kidshealth.org/kid/htbw
Do you want to learn more about how the human body works? This website provides movies, activities, and kid-friendly articles about the organs and organ systems.

"World Almanac for Kids"
www.worldalmanacforkids.com
The World Almanac for Kids supplies a lot of great information about animals, plants, famous scientists, technology, and other exciting topics.

"Your Gross and Cool Body"
http://yucky.discovery.com/flash/body/
Discover the truth about spit, burps, bad breath, earwax, and other strange happenings in the human body. This website explains the organ systems in a funny and clear way.

Become an expert

- Memorize the seven life processes: movement, reproduction, sensitivity, nutrition, excretion, respiration, and growth.

- Learn more about scientists who contributed to cell research. Look up Andreas Vesalius and his illustrations about anatomy.

- Make a chart of the organ systems (like the one on page 32). Add colorful illustrations to help you remember the important jobs of each system.

Index